Born and raised in Singapore, Jee Leong Koh moved to New York in 2003 and has lived there since. He has a First in English from Oxford University and an MFA in Creative Writing from Sarah Lawrence College. He is the curator of the website Singapore Poetry and the co-chair of the inaugural Singapore Literature Festival in New York City. This is his fifth book of poems, and the first to be published in the UK.

JEE LEONG KOH

Steep Tea

CARCANET

First published in Great Britain in 2015 by
Carcanet Press Limited
Alliance House
Cross Street
Manchester M2 7AQ

www.carcanet.co.uk

We welcome your comments on our publications
Write to us at info@carcanet.co.uk

A CIP catalogue record for this book is available from the British Library

ISBN 978184777 2275

The publisher acknowledges financial assistance from Arts Council England

Typeset by XL Publishing Services, Exmouth

For Guy

Contents

Eve's Fault 9
The Rooms I Move In 10
Found Poem 11
St Thomas Preaching in Hell's Kitchen 12
You Know, Don't You 13
The Wine Bottle Holder 14
Backache 15
A Whole History 16
Useless 17
The Xpakinté and the Drunk 18
The Clocks 19
Gorgeous Unfinished Wood Braced in Grey Iron 20
Portrait with Blue Shirt 22
For Lust 23
domed/doomed/deem'd 24
Broccoli 25
Easter 26
Quiet, please— 27
Fall: Five Poems 28
Paragraph 29
Suddenly, in Sweden 30
What the River Says 31
Kinder Feelings 32

Recognition 34
Attribution 36
Novenary with Hens 37
The Children and the Swans 38
Woodwork 39
The Hospital Lift 40
Talking to Koon Meng Who Called Himself Christopher 41
Bougainvillea 44
Ashtrays as Big as Hubcaps 45
Reversi, Also Called Othello 46
In His Other House 47
Haibun 48
Carp Swimming 49
Temple Art 50

Hong Kong   51
Black Dragon Pool   52
Dragonfly   54
Steep Tea   55
In Death As In Life   59
Singapore Buses Are Very Reliable   60
Singapore Catechism   62
Litany   63
Airplane Poems   65

Notes   67
Acknowledgements   69
Bibliography   70

Eve's Fault

Eve, whose fault was only too much love
Aemilia Lanyer, 'Salve Deus Rex Judaeorum: Eve's Apology'

God won her when he whipped out from his planetary sleeve
a bouquet of light. They watched the parade of animals pass.
He told her the joke about the Archaeopteryx, and she noted
the feathers and the lethal claws, a poem, the first of its kind.
On a beach raised from the ocean with a shout, he entered her
and she realized, in rolling waves, that love joins and separates.

The snake was a quieter fellow. He came in the fall evenings
through the long grass, his steps barely parting the blades.
Each time he showed her a different path. As they wandered,
they talked about the beauty of the light striking the birch,
the odd behavior of the ants, the fairest way to split an apple.
When Adam appeared, the serpent gave her up to happiness.

For happy was she when she met Adam under the tree of life,
still is, and Adam is still Adam, inarticulate, a terrible speller,
his body precariously balanced on his feet, his mind made up
that she is the first woman and he the first man. He needed
her and so scratched down and believed the story of the rib.
She needed Adam's need, so different from God's and the snake's,

and that was when she discovered herself outside the garden.

The Rooms I Move In

the ache of things ending in the jasmine darkening early
Eavan Boland, 'The Rooms of Other Women Poets'

I have moved in the rooms of women poets
and, seeing African violets, checked if they needed water,

careful not to disturb the stolen time in the chair,
the swivel leather seat, the high cane back.

The desk, if there was one, was bright with circumstance
cast by an Anglepoise lamp, crooked, articulate.

The window might look out on an old monastery
but the door kept its ear open to the crib.

Such rooms I move in when I move between the men
crowded with desire they disperse in a stranger's hand.

Before their face I offer the flower of my mouth,
red in the red light but also out of the red light,

a wild hibiscus impossible to label chaste
if my red mouth is not so chastened by my need.

Found Poem

Open your gates, and let me through to God.
Anna Wickham, 'Prayer to Love'

In the day room a woman stupefied from masturbation.
Another flirted with Bonaparte. A third delivered nightly
a hundred babies and in the morning killed their mouths.
A painter, once a great beauty, had rubbed all her hair out.

The troublesome idea was that you were not so different.
You recognized them as funhouse distortions of your lust,
your love of power and of babies, your aspiration for art.
The quinine, delivered in a kind tonic, queried your head.

When your husband dragged you shouting from the garden
to the confines of the house, you put a fist in the glass door.
Your poem was a symptom of madness, as was your belief
that your husband, an astronomer, did not understand you.

Now you lived in a house that arranged its barred windows
for your pleasure. Your head had not one but two doctors.
What you loved to do—singing and playing the piano—
you were encouraged to do because it was good for you.

You could have turned mad, but you spoke to the painter,
listening to her tell of a thwarted love for another woman.
You wrote to her brother about the sense she was making.
You rubbed her head with Harlene. The hair grew back.

After you were discharged, as determined by another man,
you made up your mind to be your own woman, falling
in love with an American heiress, writing, writing, writing,
keeping house for struggling writers and painters and sons.

One evening, after the war, you looked through a window
and, thinking to open the French window, hanged yourself.
It was a troublesome idea that you were not so different.
Your son, the baby, denied it, who found you in the dark.

St Thomas Preaching in Hell's Kitchen

Now at the end of her life she is all hair—
Eiléan Ní Chuilleanáin, 'St Mary Magdalene Preaching at Marseilles'

Near the end of his life, his face is all eyes
and his hands two blisters.
Still he demands to see in order to believe,
to hold a joint as it burns.

In restaurants servers think
they are actors in disguise. They practice
their French by reciting the specials.
They reappear at the right moment.

Tourists hope they are enjoying themselves.
They giggle at the sex shops, they google ABC News,
they photograph Ripley's Believe It
or Not.

Bars are crowded with loneliness, the buzz
between drink and drunk.
Men grow old here,
without giving each other more than a glance.

Thomas knows them, the servers and the lovers.
They hurry past him preaching on the street
or laugh into his owlish face.
When they curse him,

he knows, they will soon beg him
to lay his blisters on their heads.
Not the tourists. They see his swollen eyes
and drop a coin in his tin.

You Know, Don't You

They are fugitives. Intimates of myth.
Eavan Boland, 'Listen. This is the Noise of Myth'

This is the story of a man and a man,
not found in Eden, perhaps in Uruk,
but really in a bar at Second Avenue
and East Houston, near the F train stop.

You know how it goes. Fabulous Uruk,
a bar called Urge, a train that curses,
but I should tell you the separate ways
they got there, what they told themselves.

One story had to do with nervous flight
from a golden perch in a gilded cage.
The ocean in the other tale released
the fisherman, and he broke surface.

These stories they told each other at the bar,
comparing notes, harmonizing tones, so
the stories that began with 'I' and 'me'
found, in their telling, temporary company.

Listen, they're asking where the other lives.
They're edging their stories past the past
and making them up presently as they leave
the bar. What do they think they're doing?

I don't know. The waves rise again and crash
over them, as they flag down a cruising cab.
The torrential air, invisible and powerful,
drives them in, and slams the door after them.

The Wine Bottle Holder

I know the names for the flowers
they were but not the shape they made
                    Eavan Boland, 'The Wild Spray'

From Paris you brought back your first gift
for me, a stainless steel wine holder, curv-
ing in a single arch, seen from the side,
and, from the top, a shiny sharp-edged plane.

It was the most defined thing in my kitchen
where mismatched mugs squatted in the sink,
the gas cooker was bronzed with spits of sauce,
and ripe bananas hung over the trash.

I stashed it in some cupboard and forgot
those early days of careful give-and-take.
Now, taking out the holder from my mind,
and flashing it, this way, that, in the sun,

I see it keeps its clear and severe lines,
the boundaries of being, and within
the first material it is made of,
the graceful arch supporting still a bridge,

but, more, the months have worn its cutlass shine
to a glow, cutlery's, and here it sits,
its empty mouth also a steady hand,
to hold the bottle of Bordeaux we choose.

Backache

Every part of us
alerts another part.
        Kay Ryan, 'Chinese Foot Chart'

Back when we were
together, me rubbing
your shoulders, my
cock would press
against my shorts
in sympathy. My
pulse would sprint
to kiss the tips of
your strong fingers
caressing my scalp.
How strange that
morning, crawling
out of bed in pain,
you complained of
heartburn and I felt
nothing, helpless to
stop the nerve of us
from coming apart.

A Whole History

In the morning they were both found dead.
Of cold. Of hunger. Of the toxins of a whole history.
Eavan Boland, 'Quarantine', Section IV of 'Marriage'

The floor is cold with the coming winter.
     I pull on white socks
and sit down before the blackout window
to think about our separation closing in.

We have a history longer than the two years
     that fitted like a shirt.
You learned a long time ago to enjoy ironing.
I always had someone ironing shirts for me.

But we go further back than birth, to furtive
     park encounters,
coded glances, tapping on bathroom walls,
ways of staying warm and white in winter.

Yesterday a young friend said it's wrong
     to expose children
to a gay wedding. The chill hit me again.
Rage spread like blood over my clean shirt.

I cannot wash it off. You are no longer willing.
     In the closet the shirt,
part reminder of love, part reminder of rage,
is held up by its shoulders on thin twisted wire.

Useless

To see for the first time a thing other
than the mire of food
Lee Tzu Pheng, 'Neanderthal Bone Flute: A Discovery'

When she was sucking the bone clean of marrow
at a feast thrown by him for his now woman,
when his now woman snuggled close up to him,
smacking her lips over the bone he'd picked for her,
when everyone agreed what a great feast it was
and congratulated her for being the birth reason,
when she said, in reply, that just four days ago
they had celebrated their third together year,

the once woman put her bone away. For two months
he lay with his now woman before he left her.
She had no words for this useless discovery.
The whole night the marrow bubbled in her mouth.

The Xpakinté and the Drunk

The Xpakinté is not really a person,
although she looks like a woman.
Munda Tostó, 'The Xpakinté', translated from Tzotzil by Ámbar Past

He is walking on a writhing snake   but isn't.
The moon is down with pox   but isn't.

A light is shining by the bank of mists   but isn't.
The light is running from the Xpakinté   but isn't.

She looks like a woman   but isn't.
She looks like his wife, her hair braided with red pompons, but isn't.

She is calling him from her long throat   but isn't.
She loses her shawl and skirt, and shows coiled flesh   but isn't.

Her skin is rough as bark   but isn't.
Her cunt is stuffed with leaves   but isn't.

The tree is crawling with hairy caterpillars   but isn't
and stings like fire   but isn't.

In the morning he is found dead   but isn't.
He is home with his wife, the pretty one with red pompons in
                                                                            her hair.

The Clocks

I make a trip to each clock in the apartment
Elizabeth Bishop, 'Paris, 7 A.M.'

One clock is squat. Another is a dog
that bounds around every twelve years and barks
at dogs not yet born and dogs gone before.
The good clock in the kitchen is a white soup bowl.
The one I check to keep up with New York
vibrates in my pocket, next to my penis,
or rings with a ringtone called Wizard.

So many clocks! How does one keep time?
I have been in love thrice. The first
is sleeping in my bed, a visitor whirring softly.
The second stopped the minute
the *Mayflower* docked. The third is striking
fifty-one today. He sounds sad.
How do I sound to him?
How do I sound in his tall apartment of clocks?
My collection of clocks
in that apartment, and that apartment, and that apartment?

First visit to an airport, I was rapt by the world clocks,
Jakarta, New Delhi, Tel Aviv, Berlin, London, New York,
steel round-faced timekeepers, all different and all right,
their hands ringing in my ears
the sound of a wet finger rubbing the rim of a water glass,
and I felt like a dog that was trying to catch its tail.
Dizzy, yes, but filled with so much joy
I think I have not left the spot.

Gorgeous Unfinished Wood Braced in Grey Iron

Save us from being devoured by the new thatch
or the shiny nails.

Xunka' Utz'utz' Ni', 'So the New House Won't Eat Us',
translated from Tzotzil by Ámbar Past

They are eating us, the lamps dangling like fruit
from curvy metal stems
that sucked up days of browsing catalogues,

the Sony 24" HDTV and the media console,
gorgeous unfinished wood braced in grey iron,
that cost more than we thought,

the witchy bedroom blinds
that can be lowered from the top or raised from the ledge
to stop curious eyes,

the kitchen cart, the black bookshelves,
the dish drainer, the shower caddy, the vacuum cleaner,
the plastic food containers that swallow each other like Russian dolls.

Close the mouths of the envious, *Kajval,*
shut up the scolding socialists.
Let the hermit crawl back to his hole.

We will pray to the spirit in things,
we will pray to you, *Kajval,* Mother,
Earth,

turning first, with clasped hands, to the fading photo
of sister, husband and baby Hannah
on the black bookshelf,

turning next to the dining table
that father Norval built from cherry wood
and you, love, drove for nine hours across four states from Cincinnati,

and add our prayers to those of the Mayan lady,
who is poor beyond our imagination,
but tallies our hearts:

Let the saints in their coffers,
the voices that speak from inside old chests,
stand up for those who live in this house.

Portrait with Blue Shirt

Our expressions are too earnest and naïve
Zhang Er, 'NuChou (Ugly Girl)',
translated from Chinese by Susan M. Schultz

Alert, open,
the face has not
yet learned
to protect its look
from the world.

A sharp blow
—losing a foot
or acquiring
an incurable
failure—
will close it.

The face knows
its luck
will not hold.
It waits
for fate's knuckles

but is not
ready (it is
a young face)
for the
slow crack
of age.

for Valerie, who painted me

For Lust

But for lust we could be friends
Ruth Pitter, 'But for Lust'

I want to call you back but do not think I should.
I am in love now, you see, and love must exclude
its lookalikes, its foreign gods, its counterproof.
He is so good to me and when I am not good
he calmly rubs away what in my soul is rough.
Approve may rhyme with love, but so does disapprove.

But o the nights of passion you and I had shared,
the baring of the places that we thought were bared,
re-slotting what was present into what was past,
no holds barred, no forbidden gestures, nothing spared.
I will not call you back although I feel I must.
Trust rhymes with lust, but, my desire, so does distrust.

domed/doomed/deem'd

Soe some pleasure shadowe-like is wrought
Lady Mary Wroth, 'Pamphilia to Amphilanthus'

This reading light on the poems of Lady Mary Wroth
is like a spot of consciousness. It decodes the marks,
grievous and oddly spelled, as in *domed* for *doomed*,
straightens out the urgent inversions, reconstructs
the labyrinth of sense into the sonnet's concert hall
and drops out of sight as the music rises, subsides.

Just beyond is darkness. Unseen, in the next room,
you finalize your drawing of the church restoration.
You said before, you love to know that I am near,
hearing the couch sighing, or smelling my coffee,
whereas, lost in my poetry books, I turn oblivious
to your presence, and so you feel outside of love.

Dear, you may be outside the circle of my thought
but not the influence of love. When Mary Wroth
sings out, *The knowing part of joye is deem'd the hart*,
she means a great part is redeemed by unknowing.
I am more than the heart, more than a reading light,
this coffee, this sighing, this darkness, is love too.

Broccoli

Does the mundane appear as a man in my dreams because I am a woman?
Kimura Nobuko, 'Mundaneness', translated from Japanese by Hiroaki Sato

I think, I am going to get out of bed, and I get out of bed.
In the middle of the day, I think, I have been here before.

I live like a man in a dream that a woman is dreaming,
dreaming of the appearance of the mundane.
One day I will smash the plates to wake her up.

Now I watch myself shaving broccoli off their stalks, scattering
tiny, tiny green florets over cutting board, counter, floor,
no matter how gently I wield the knife.

Easter

your body an arrival
you know is false but can't outrun
                    Jorie Graham, 'The Geese'

The manufacturers have dropped the on button
from their gizmos, or else have made
the on button also the off button. Every day
is full of indignities. Light wash, normal wash.
Back to front. Push to turn.

The beautiful spring day in the park
proves the forecast wrong. It's worrying.
The baby stroller threads the submerged
rocks. The tulips dazzle all of us,
four men and two women. Normal wash,
heavy wash.

The woman who grew up with grandmother
played house alone in Florida.
The other children visited in the winter,
when there was no flooding.
The woman with breast cancer announces
her medication has made her menopausal.
She's the one pushing her daughter and looking
for the bathroom.

There are only ever two women.

Heavy wash, light wash. Back home,
you remove the dirty dishes from the broken cycle.
You look up flights to Paris.
You check all the cheap fare websites and they give
the same price for summer.

for Lynn and Robyn

Quiet, please—

Why did you bring me here?
Sara Teasdale, 'Coney Island'

the beach is turning over to sleep, drawing up

to its shoulders the slipping blanket of the sea.

The old Ferris wheel is slowing to a final stop,

its wooden cars empty. The stands are closing.

On the pier, extended like a promise, the lines

are reeled back to their hollow round casings.

The patrol boat is circling an invisible crater

      as if someone is drowning.

Fall: Five Poems

When we stumble over a stone
It guides us.

Suzan Alaiwan, 'Poems', translated
from Arabic by Sayed Gouda

He listens for the stumble in a poem, so he can find the stone.

On a white stone is scribbled this short poem: I stumbled.

When you stumble over a stone, do not pocket the stone.

I do not say, O poem, you are stone, but I say you are home.

Here, take this stone: may it be to you a guide and a poem.

Paragraph

It made the children laugh and play,
To see a lamb at school.
          Sarah Josepha Hale, 'Mary's Lamb'

I tell my VI graders my favorite word is *freedom*.
It is a house with many rooms on a lazy afternoon,
and outside the house an overgrown path runs
to the woods, where a speckled stream giggles.
I tell them *freedom* is made up of two syllables.
The first sounds like the neighing of a runaway
horse, unbridled muscles in his voice. The second
echoes like a blow on the taut skin of a tom-tom.
And freedom, as all musicians and writers know,
is impossible without the discipline of the drum.
My students are impressed by my improvisation.
They buckle down to writing their paragraph.
I look out the window of this old school building
and there's the river, sun-lit, a tidal strait really,
heading toward the sea. I don't tell them the sea.
Or what becomes of a carthorse with no master.
Or an abandoned house. I gently strike the drum.

for Patty

29

Suddenly, in Sweden

O the chimneys
Nelly Sachs, 'O the chimneys',
translated from German by Michael Roloff

The very tall chimney on the very tall building
has been glumly silent all winter.
This morning, finally, it has something to say for itself.

Whatever it says
shoots up so quickly that it is lost in the space
behind the sky.

The black smoke flies after it, haltingly,
then spreads out like a net
that catches nothing but its own unknotting.

I say net, but it could have been hair.
I say sky, but it was a handcart of discarded clothes.
I say silent, but the chimney has been speaking in German all winter.

What the River Says

The body is a source. Nothing more.
                    Eavan Boland, 'Anna Liffey'

I too compare my life frequently to a river,
small hidden beginning, final dissolution,
body charged with a name but always changing.

It is a place to live by, to keep a few chickens
or raise a city famous for its graceful bridges,
if one cares for good eating or reaching across.

On mornings when the rear courtyard is stony,
how enjoyable to walk to the water and hear
gossip about young lovers parting upstream.

The annual swelling is a power for great evil
but also a pregnancy. It carries boats and people.
For frenzy, there is a waterfall round the corner.

Most vitalizing is the promise of plunging in,
to drop the half-sensed world with its fatal air
and experience total absolution in an instant.

So, if my body is a river, I won't dismiss it
as a source and nothing more. It is a source
of my voice but it is also my voice: the river

is what the river says on its way to the sea.

Kinder Feelings

So crowded here, Grand Central Terminal, people pouring
along the greatest number of train platforms in the world
(with a secret platform to whisk a President with polio
to the Waldorf-Astoria) to the Main Concourse, swirling
around the stones of tourists—moved unsurely by the rush—
dividing in intelligent streams into various passageways,
as if separated by an industrious chemist, Mercury perhaps.

So different from the one station in Singapore (one station!)
where on the walls rice is planted, rubber tapped, tin mined,
activities that happened, are happening, elsewhere, not there,
and on the platform waiting for the train I watched the grass
burn between the railway ties, between the broken stones,
imagined miles of railway tracks crisscrossing everywhere
and stones rising to wing the helm of travel's cathedral.

Now I am here, brought not by dream but engineering,
my eyes recording images my mind will work on later,
my body filling up with energy from bodies in friction,
and though tempted to disavow the broken ties of home
I look back at the kitsch with kinder feelings, learn to look
for Singapore in train timetables, at the information booth
with the four-faced clock, each face a trembling opal.

for Eric

ॐ

Recognition

a duck that would not lay
and a runt of a papaya tree
Lee Tzu Pheng, 'My Country and My People'

Did you grow a bean plant
as a school science project,
noting carefully in a jotter
book the stages of growth
that a dark green textbook
taught? They did not say,
the books, what to do with
a fully-grown bean plant,
and so I reluctantly threw
it down the rubbish chute,
feeling bad at the thought
of leaves squelched with
gum, hair, chicken bones,
the slender white stalk
bent. Did you dig a hole
in the schoolyard secretly
and plant an orange pip,
then watch the soil keep
quiet? Did you keep chicks
(all the children did) as if
you were back in the village?
After accidentally stepping
on one to death, did you
give away the other chick
because someone told you
that it would die if it lived
alone? Did you hear that
or did you, my country-
woman, hear another say,
no one dies of loneliness?
Or did you hear both voices,
sometimes in competition
like car horns, sometimes

in counterpoint, when you
signed the divorce papers,
when the Senior Minister
in an interview regretted
sending women to school,
when you lectured on the
Romantics, remembering
the bean plant cast away
in its plastic mould, when
your daughter shifted on
your hip, when you wrote,
the home air-conditioning
clicking, humming, raising
goosebumps, a poem?

Attribution

I speak with the forked tongue of colony.
Eavan Boland, 'The Mother Tongue'

My grandfather said life was better under the British.
He was a man who begrudged his words but he did say this.

I was born after the British left
an alphabet in my house, the same book they left in school.

I was good in English.
I was the only one in class who knew 'bedridden' does not mean lazy.

I was so good in English they sent me to England
where I proved my grandfather right

until I was almost sent down for plagiarism I knew was wrong
and did not know was wrong, because where I came from
everyone plagiarized.

I learned to attribute everything I wrote.
It is not easy.

Sometimes I cannot find out who first wrote the words I wrote.
Sometimes I think I wrote the words I wrote with such delight.

Often the words I write have confusing beginnings
and none can tell what belongs to the British, my grandfather or me.

Novenary with Hens

No one is there for you. Don't call, don't cry.
Mimi Khalvati, 'Villanelle'

I couldn't count to ten till I turned eleven.
The chicks were soft and yellow. One was jet.
One, two, buckle my shoe, nine and a big fat hen.

They scratched the grass beside the shop for men.
They were the best present a boy could get.
I couldn't count to ten till I turned eleven.

Mother called out from above. That was when
I stepped back—three, two, one—and on my pet.
One, two, buckle my shoe, nine and a big fat hen.

The grass turned black. Its head was not broken.
Father could fix it but he was not home yet.
I couldn't count to ten till I turned eleven.

The Shopgirl cried out, *Poke the thing back in!*
The tiny mitten was mewing, mewing for it.
One, two, buckle my shoe, nine and a big fat hen.

My hands did what the Shopgirl said. Even then,
I couldn't save it. Now I can't forget
I couldn't count to ten till I turned eleven.
One, two, buckle my shoe, nine and a big fat hen.

The Children and the Swans

In the shaken warmth of early March
Eavan Boland, 'The Liffey beyond Islandbridge'

The swans, one black, one white,
steer in the man-made lake
the children's eyes to them,
and hoist the children's hands.

When the bread is pitched
with childish force and aim,
and the great birds bend their
heads to peck at a crumb,

the children know they've won
a prize. They can make swans
come to them. They can break
the waters. They can even fly.

Woodwork

the wedge and the hollow are imprinted on everything
Maria Isabel Barreno, Maria Teresa Horta, Maria Velho da Costa,
'Saddle and Cell', translated from Portuguese by Helen R. Lane

The wood to be turned into a door wedge
shows a pale grain and smells of incense.
Soft, like my palm, it keeps
the teeth marks of a vice closed too tight.
It shrinks from the metal lip of the plane.

The boy across the worktable
marks his job with a soft pencil.
His hands, a shade darker than the wood,
handle his work as if it is a spinning top
or a Frisbee.

The workshop hums and curves
to the same diagram,
laminated edges fraying from ghost fingers
into white hair.

Next semester we work on paint scrapers.

The Hospital Lift

The Virgin was spiralling to heaven,
Hauled up in stages. Past mist and shining
Eiléan Ní Chuilleanáin, 'Fireman's Lift'

My mother is the aged Queen of the spin
of washing machines. Her body sags now
but when she was young-eyed and toned
she washed St Andrew's Children's Hospital,
whose best feature was its ancient lift.

I would close the brass grille with a clang,
thump the big black top button, grow up
watching the concrete floors drop to my feet,

the bowl that glowed in underwater green

the babies crying, startled by the light

in blue gowns the boys chasing the clown

the professional look of clean white smocks

before arriving on the roof, the sky
smelling of detergent, wind and sun,
the wash flapping like giant birds.

When my mother turned to greet me
with a tight smile (now loosening indefinitely),
how was I to catch the sleight of hand
that hoisted through space a wonderful lift
by spinning dirty sheets and pillowslips?

Talking to Koon Meng Who
Called Himself Christopher

I sing one stanza to my lute and a Tartar horn.
Cai Yan, '18 Verses Sung to a Tartar Reed Whistle',
translated from Chinese by Kenneth Rexroth and Ling Chung

Having been thrashed by the Express boys
in soccer, we retreated to the canteen.
You sitting with a foot up on the bench
challenged them, 'Basketball tomorrow, we
sure won't lose. All-Star China versus England.'

Ben smiled and said, 'Whenever', to me, 'Thanks, Sir,
for playing. A good game,' and left for class.

Jin Sheng, who christened himself Nicholas,
yawned loudly, 'School so *xian*, so boring, ah-h-h.'

In the still air, you spoke your thoughts aloud,
'You know what, T'cher, I miss the Express class
by four points only,' holding up four fingers.
'In prim'ry school, I very good boy one.
I every day go home and study hard,
practice my math, believe or not.'

                              Jin snorted.

You cast a sidelong glance at me before
continuing, 'But I did not make it, so
I turn bad. Sometimes got caught, *ganna* caned.
We run round in class, never sit down one.'
No one could stop you. When they sent you out,
'We feel dem proud, laugh and walk out like nothing.
If I do very well and get five As
and behave, can I still go Express now?'

'No.' I explained, 'They take different subjects.'

41

'I miss by four points only, now can't change.
English last time no good.'

              'T'cher, he like Shirlene',
Jin sniggered. 'You know her? From Three Express.'

'I taught her in Sec. One. She did quite well
and moved from Normal to Express. She's nice.'

'See, people very smart one. You no hope.'

'Who say no hope? Maybe we meet in Poly.'

Remembering my teacher's pledge, I said,
'That's right. Do well in your Four N exam,
go study what you like at ITE,
do very well there and you can then go
to Polytechnic. It just takes a little
longer,' anticipating your objection.

You said nothing. You lay down on the bench,
sighed very loudly and stared at the ceiling.
'School very *xian*', you said at last.

               The bell.

'What period now?'

           'Shit. Civics,' Jin Sheng said.

'That arsehole Mr. Mah. I have no book,
sure *ganna* scolding one. Whole period. Fuck.'
You peeked at me and quoted with a smirk,
'We use vulgarities a lot because
we have a limited vocabulary,
right, T'cher?'

          Before I could reach for an answer,
you stood up, stretched and sauntered back to class.

The canteen grew quiet enough to hear
you in my head, without the need to translate
into imperfectly received pro-NOUN-
see-A-shen curses at your gain and loss.
My Caliban, I thought, hurrying to
Lit class, *Galatea or...*

                     Your voice challenged,
'What, T'cher?' and I answered, 'Christopher.'

Bougainvillea

... *the heart*
can sometimes be troublesome.

Lee Tzu Pheng, 'Singapore River'

When the island is starved for a hymn,
this land of bougainvillea, illegible graves, and car dealerships,
where eating has usurped the offices of sex,
where sun is oppressively silent and rain everywhere gossips,

as the ear remembers one musical phrase, we clutch our name,
sung by a long-dead mother, beyond a deaf father's reach,
and agonize over eating our name
or planting it in the beach.

We look over the wall to see what our neighbors do.
Their garden is smooth as a pair of jeans.
They look as hungry as yesterday.
When they greet us, they sound obscene.

Shall we eat it? We are so hungry.
It will recall the satisfactions of lying with a woman or a man.
No! We must plant it.
But what if our name does not grow songs in sand?

The bougainvillea puts out pink and purple flowers, rice paper-thin.
The graves settle back defeated by air.
The cars exchange hands like trophies.
The sun is silent oppressively and the rain gossips everywhere.

Ashtrays as Big as Hubcaps

In the women's restroom, one compartment stood open.
A woman knelt there, washing something in the white bowl.
                                    Mary Oliver, 'Singapore'

That woman scrubbing the big ashtrays with a blue rag,
she was my mother. Her hands were not moving like a river.
Her dark hair was not like the wing of a bird, it was wispy.
When she smiled at you, she was not feeling embarrassed.
The toilet bowl was a handy place to wash the big ashtrays
but she guessed the work argued with your wobbly stomach.

You flew home and put her in a poem called 'Singapore'.
I don't doubt for a moment that she loves her life, you wrote,
I want her to rise up from the slop and fly down to the river.
She becomes, for you and your American fans, a picture
of *the light that can shine out of a life,* meaning, a saint,
and the picture is completed, roundly, with trees and birds.

She bused home and said nothing, for you were forgotten
in her rush to stick the laundry out of the windows to dry.
She remembered you later, the night as humid as always.
She had nice stockings on, or else she could have knelt
in my place. She must have troubles of her own, we all do,
she said, with the resentful condescension of the poor.

Reversi, Also Called Othello

no matter how many turns
you make

Lee Tzu Pheng, 'Tough, Love'

Flip over a black
lie to white. Flip
coffee in a diner
mug. Flip 1ˢᵗ sight.

Flip a coin. Flip girls
and boys. Flip and
then flip back black
light. White noise.

Flip a ship on its
side. Flip two sides.
Flip the living and
the dead just died.

Flip dark hair on
pale shin. Flip a
treasured negative.
Flip a safety pin.

In His Other House

In this house there is no need to wait for the verdict of history
And each page lies open to the version of every other.
                    Eiléan Ní Chuilleanáin, 'In Her Other House'

In my other house too, books fill the floor-to-ceiling shelves,
not only books on stock markets, seven habits, ghost stories,
but also poetry, Arthur Yap, Cyril Wong, Alfian Sa'at,
and one who moved away and who wrote *Days of No Name*.

My father comes home from the power station. When rested
(and this is how I know this is not real) he reads to us again,
for the seventh time, Philip Jeyaretnam's *Abraham's Promise*
in a quiet voice, unbroken by a frightened young supervisor.

When he closes the book, my dead grandfather stirs heavily
and says a word or two, that really says he has been listening.
And my beloved, knowing his cue, jumps up from the couch
to clear the dishes, for, he says, dishes don't wash themselves.

Softly brightened by a feeling I do not hurry to identify,
I move to the back of him and put my arms around his waist.
His muscles twitch like the needle on a motorboat's dashboard
as he turns a bone china plate against a rough cotton cloth.

The light from the window looks like a huge, blank sea.
In this other house there will be time to fill it but right now
the bell intones in silver, and here, on a surprise night visit,
are my sister and her two daughters coming through the door.

Haibun

A son should do more, but you do not stop talking about the one
time I took you and dad on a vacation. You could have asked to
visit anywhere, New York, Paris, Beijing. You chose the cheap old
glamour of Penang. When you were a child, your great-uncle told
you of the night bazaars, blazing with kerosene lanterns, which
sold everything from leather luggage bags to a bowl of laksa. Your
cousins returned from another visit to the island, complaining
that they didn't go anywhere special, but loaded with postcards,
sweetmeats and trinkets. You kept for years the pearl earrings in
their tiny bag of clear plastic. You didn't have them anymore when
we stood on the highest point of Penang, the cloudy city below our
feet, the caged birds in our ears. With a laugh, you asked me to take
a photograph of you holding a tendril of a vine drooping from a
wooden trellis. You posed demurely, like some film star in the fifties.
Your eyes half-closed, you looked into my camera.

    Stirring the goldfish bowl with her finger, she lights the small
hurricane lamps.

Carp Swimming

this dissension into fish or birds
dg nanouk okpik, 'For-The-Spirits-Who-Have-Rounded-The-Bend'

Because I can look for hours at carp swimming,
red lightning, finny torpedo,
although bullfrogs croak for a groggy season,
and mosquitoes breed irritation into fever,
Aedes mosquitoes, flying rats, carriers
of breakbone fever, water poison,
although the Chinese water snake, crepuscular in his habit,
                                                    olive brown,
'a longitudinal stripe of dark salmon extending from head to tail',
is hunted and killed for manufacturing snake oil
to cure arthritis, killed for being useful,
because I can stare for whole days at carp swimming,
although the willows bend their heads and cry
for god knows what,
because I can look at carp swimming
and see the lightning,
I have hope that I will survive the bullfrogs, the mosquitoes,
and even the snares of snake-oil makers,
the hooked nets of usefulness,
because I can look at carp,
my gracious quarrel with the world,
I will survive the depredations of the spirit
and live in what I saw,
because I can look for hours at carp swimming,
and because I see the kingfisher dart into his kill.

after Hyam Plutzik

Temple Art

from here to the base of the statue is quite a long way
Diana Bridge, 'Sequence, Sarnath'

The scorpion, ink-black,
    looks out
        from his muscled back,
    its eyes pierced
and piercing, its tail
        poised to strike.

How like the temple guardians
    of China.
        With sure violence,
    invisible noise,
they leave in you
        a grit, the lions.

Look too long at scorpion jet
    and you
        are left
    with a drop of poison:
you are in the forecourt.
        This is as far as you get.

for Katherine H.

50

Hong Kong

some curio of the change
Lee Tzu Pheng, 'Prospect of a Drowning'

We found him among the small antique shops
in the Soho district of Hong Kong. Below
Buddha posters and beside porcelain MJ

stood at smart attention a terracotta soldier,
an officer of some rank, the height of my hand.
Factory plaster had been painted a gritty grey

and in the hair pulled back to show a broad
forehead, in the protective vest, in the folds
of his sleeves and in the creases of his shoes,

a brown as fine and light as sand, as if he had
just been rescued from a centuries-old grave.
He was a lovely copy, meticulous, affordable,

but we were searching for a Mao statuette
for Di and Ty. The only keepsake I wanted,
memories, not postcards or knickknacks,

I insisted, to myself. You urged me to get him.
You knew better than to keep me to my word
when my hands weighed him again. Now he

stands guard by my laptop, eyes unblinking,
under a moustache a steady serious mouth,
keeping as best as he can the past perfect.

Black Dragon Pool

I have no words for my weary sorrow
Li Qingzhao, 'On Plum Blossoms', translated from
Chinese by Kenneth Rexroth and Ling Chung

You showed me the verses
Du Fu wrote, deep in poverty,

unappreciated by the court,
unhappy with his lot.

I remember only the image
of an unlit stove.

What impressed me more
was that you copied

his poem into your book,
and other poets of loss,

pages of neat handwriting,
after your daughter died.

Almost unrelated
came the thought

of Black Dragon Pool
in the city of Lijiang,

last summer,
a cloudless sky,

how I was unsure
if the people prayed to the gods

to stop the dragon
from drinking up the water,

or prayed to the dragon
or to the pool.

for Katherine S.

Dragonfly

Trying to escape its own fire a firefly dies
   Yamada Mizue, translated from Japanese by Hiroaki Sato

Motorcyclist of the air, look out
for summer, the roar of flies
dangling like daredevils from wings.
You too are a devil, serpent, but fly
at full stretch, with deadly purpose,
at accidents. Look out for ponds,
frogs' hunting ground. Throttle back,
release. See water boil noiselessly.
This is how all life began and you
beget too, a Levitical line. Dragon,
look out for the significant detail
of yourself, goggle eyes, the long
but useless legs, the Indian shape,
a cross with two horizontal bars,
the top for the nails, the lower,
slightly larger, for powering up.

Steep Tea

an autumn kasen renga, written with Rachael Briggs
25 August–11 September 2012

maple, apple
steep the world in red
we sip jewel tea

> the fire temple disappears
> a watery moon

chili dip
on a seaweed cracker
thesis antithesis crunch

> oral defence
> visiting mum in Syracuse

cherry blossoms
artillery that liquefies in my hand
… or was it snow?

> re-categorized from 4C to 442
> swear allegiance to …

(le) poisson rouge
Taka Kigawa
plays *Die Kunst der Fuge*

> alien fauna of George Street
> a kangaroo with gears for ears

you on the
exercise bike, come share
my yoga mat

> can we be Lion and Thunderbolt,
> Hero and King Dancer?
> I'm in!

Fujisan from far away
the dance
before the dance

                              my skipping stone cavorts
                              between dust and river bottom

traveler's moon
cools her tired feet
in a red basin

                              uh-oh tiptoe possum
                              oh no stolen plum

hot off the press
New Jersey doctor delivers
new verse

                              Greyhound bus to Rutgers
                              the Syracuse University of
                                             New Brunswick

impossible boys
hardy, kind and smart
chrysanthemums in winter

                              in juvenile hall
                              we snuck a sunbeam through
                                             the metal detector

twigs and fluff
in the boarded-up window
also an egg

                              he's writing a book of poems
                              on women poets

what's she knitting
in the seminar, with all those twists?
a conclusive argument

                    loopy loop
                    the clock rings 5 o'clock

school's out!
Teacher sets down his pencil
grabs a frisbee

                    this summer Bali
                    next summer Kyoto, yes?

Ishihara's confections
wax, horsehair, foam
garnish with kushi

                    strand of hair on the pillow
                    drop of ice cream on his thigh

Sunday
breakfast in bed with my lover
plus or minus breakfast

                    Jesus I love you
                    no longer (x2)

bitter moon sighs
over false Solomon's seal
no more berries

                    the first fall wind, he says
                    a spirit, almost

rainclouds
did not rain on Labor Day
no thunder either

                    'I don't care if the sun don't shine'
                    she swings off key

overdub-dub-dub
a woman in a tub
The Singin' Rage

                    goddess, sing the inflammation
                                of my Achilles tendon
                    rowers are back on the Charles,
                        and I tried to sprint beside them

let's run to the tidal basin
tomorrow
to view the cherry blossoms

                    the first wild strawberry
                    invites the hummingbirds to lunch

In Death As In Life

In some city, Trieste or Udine…
Pier Paolo Pasolini, 'The Day of My Death',
translated from Italian by Mary di Michele

Your mother wants her body
donated to science, she wants
    to be useful
in death as she is in life,
    to brain,
      eye, uterus,
and even skin researchers.
She wants to be all used up.

We are more selfish. You wish
    to be cremated
and for your ash to dash across
    the Great Lawn
    we live by,
lift off like a warm grey scarf
    before landing
on grass you have traveled to.

I surprise myself by wishing
    my ash dispersed
over the sea south of Singapore,
the country I have left behind.
    That's too far,
    you complain.
It's not, I say. Come August
I'll show you the exact spot.

Singapore Buses Are Very Reliable

And they told him that in Prague his mother died.
Polina Barskova, 'Motherhood and Childhood', translated
from Russian by Boris Dralyuk and David Stromberg

She will tell me that she has died.
She won't let anyone else
call me from Singapore.

She will tell me first that my father
has seen the lung specialist
and thinned his blood,

that Fourth Aunt,
diagnosed with breast cancer,
refuses to eat,

that Raymond, my brother-in-law,
is going for minor heart surgery,
or so he says. The girls are okay.

Finally she will tell me that she fell
from a bus, like the time
when her eyes were bruised for weeks,

but this morning she couldn't get up
right away. She had reached
for the handrail, as I had urged,

but closed her fist
on air,
like that day long ago

when crossing Orchard Road
I snatched my hand from hers,
for I was going to be six.

Sorrow sorrow and sorrow.
She will compare one day to another.
That's what the dead do.

Singapore Catechism

Laterite roots
Leong Liew Geok, 'Exiles Return'

You go where?
I'm going from the literal to the lateral, from roots to routes.

You go where?
I'm going from the lateral to the littoral, from routes to riots.

You go where?
I'm going from the littoral to the literate, from riots to rights.

You go where?
I'm going from the literate to the lottery, from rights to rates.

You go where?
I'm going from the lottery to the latterly, from rates to writs

You go where?
I'm going from the latterly to the litany, from writs to rites.

You go where?
I'm going from the litany to the laterite, from rites to roots.

Litany

What is the promise of the infant year
Charlotte Smith, 'The Emigrants: A Poem [Disillusion with the French Revolution]'

Let this year be a year better than the last,
the months twelve disciples at supper, one a traitor and accomplice
                                        of the Lord,
the weeks a triumph of life, met by love, crowned by rest,
the days awarded each day with a watermelon and a word.

Let the sky be a glass of water, and the sea a plate of fried fish.
Let the man thin with thought drink and eat,
and, if it's her wish,
let the woman plump with worries diet.

In our travels, let the train arrive on time, and, if that's impossible,
                                        let the train
not trip over the track.
In our work, let the ropes hold tight, and, when the tower rises again,
let the ropes go slack.

Let our love be as our travel and our work,
earning a common currency here on Earth.
Let passion be the night dreams of a small-town clerk.
Let young love be full of eyes, and let old love be full of teeth.

A year is too brief to empty prison camps, so let a few go free.
A year is long enough for a change of heart.
Let hearts recover liberty.
Let camps be broken by candlelight.

Let the soul learn it is nothing without the body,
and the body learn it is not alone
among the rousing rose, oratorical orchid and lilting lily
the world grows in its spiral garden.

Let this year not be a decade better, for that hope would not be
                                                            serious,
not a day better, for that would be too much like the past,
and not a year worse, for that would be to go in reverse,
but let this year be a year better than the last.

Airplane Poems

I have only now become acquainted with the meaning of migration.
Yasmeen Hameed, 'I Am Still Awake',
translated from Urdu by Waqas Khwaja

You said, every Singapore poet has an airplane poem.
Takeoff. Ascent. Window view. Turbulence. Landing.
We are a race of travelers and write what we know,
the illusion of reaching and leaving easily anywhere,
the airplane, in the language of logistics, an airbridge.

Belting up, on my annual flight to Singapore, I think,
migration is the opposite of travel. It initiates a break
that one tries to stuff with one's body, like a psycho
pushing the bag of his victim into the trunk of his car.
Or one tries it with flowers, a paper cone of gerberas

lighting the edge of the grave of every vanished place.
Or else with airplane poems. For years I would fall asleep
the moment the plane took off and sleep until landing.
Not any more. The belt pinches. The seat constricts.
I'm kept awake by the cabin lights and the body aching.

for Ruihe

Notes

Found Poem
Most of the details and some of the phrasings of the poem were found in *Anna Wickham: A Poet's Daring Life* by Jennifer Vaughan Jones (Madison Books, 2003).

Paragraph
The sounds of the word 'freedom' were compared to a horse neighing and a drum playing in a book on poetry that I read in my teens. I would gladly credit the author if the information is brought to my attention.

Talking to Koon Meng Who Called Himself Christopher
In secondary school, Singapore students are assigned to one of three ability tracks, or streams, called Express, Normal (Academic), and Normal (Technical). There are limited opportunities to move between tracks. ITE (Institute of Technical Education) is where most Normal (Technical) students go for vocational training.

In His Other House
Boey Kim Cheng, a Singapore-born poet who migrated to Australia, wrote the book of poems *Days of No Name*.

Carp Swimming
The quotation about the Chinese water snake is modified from the website *Snakes of Taiwan* (www.snakesoftaiwan.com).

Steep Tea
In its last war against Japan, the USA categorized Japanese Americans as 4C (enemy aliens) and interned them. When the country needed combatants, many Japanese Americans volunteered despite the internment of their family, and as the 442nd Infantry Regiment fought with distinction in Italy and France.

Taka Kigawa, a Japanese pianist living in New York City, gave a memorable performance of Bach's *The Art of Fugue* at (le) poisson rouge.

Christopher Trotter made the scrap metal kangaroos in Brisbane. The plaque for the public sculpture says that *City Roos* symbolizes the importance of sharing space and communication.

Rachael Briggs: 'I picked the yoga poses with the most romantic and inspiring names'—Lion, Thunderbolt, Hero and King Dancer.

The New Jersey doctor and poet is William Carlos Williams.

Rachael Briggs: 'Tetsuo Ishihara's hairstyle museum is small, but it is also my favorite thing in Kyoto. Incidentally, Ishihara is unusual for his chosen occupation: almost all hairdressers for geisha are female.'

The song 'I Don't Care if the Sun Don't Shine' was recorded by Patti Page, who was promoted as the Singin' Rage. She was the first artist to overdub her vocals in a song, due to a strike by backing singers.

Acknowledgements

I am immensely grateful, for instruction and pleasure, to the poets whom I encountered variously in a single poem or a larger body of work, and to their editors, translators, anthologists, biographers and publishers. A list of their work is given in the bibliography, along with the page on which they are quoted.

My gratitude also to Helaine L. Smith, Andrew Howdle, Eric Norris and Tara Safronoff for their invaluable comments on a draft of this book. To Guy E. Humphrey, for his love.

I thank the editors of the following journals for publishing these poems, some in earlier versions:

Axon: 'Useless', 'Recognition' and 'Reversi, Also Called Othello'
The Brownstone Poets Anthology: 'The Children and the Swans'
Drunken Boat: 'Carp Swimming', 'Black Dragon Pool', 'In Death As In Life' and 'Singapore Catechism'
The Flea: 'Litany' ('Let This Year')
Kin: 'Temple Art'
Mascara: 'The Clocks (The Bowl)', 'The Hospital Lift' and 'In His Other House'
PN Review: 'Attribution', 'The Rooms I Move In', 'A Whole History', 'What the River Says', 'Ashtrays as Big as Hubcaps' and 'Kinder Feelings'
Pirene's Fountain: 'Fall: Five Poems' ('Five Poems')
Poems of Romance: 'You Know, Don't You'
Quarterly Literary Review of Singapore: 'Haibun' and 'Singapore Buses Are Very Reliable'
Scythe: 'Woodwork' and 'St Thomas Preaching in Hell's Kitchen'
Softblow: 'The Wine Bottle Holder' and 'Airplane Poems'
This Assignment Is So Gay: LGBTIQ poets on the art of teaching: 'Paragraph' and 'Talking to Koon Meng Who Called Himself Christopher'
tongues of the ocean: 'Eve's Fault'
Villanelles (Everyman's Library): 'Novenary with Hens'

Also, the editors of the following publications for reprinting these poems:

New Poetries V: 'Attribution', 'A Whole History' and 'The Rooms I Move In'
The Margins: 'Eve's Fault'
Umbrella: 'The Children and the Swans'

Bibliography

Numbers in parenthesis indicate the pages on which the poet is quoted.

Alaiwan, Suzan, in *Not A Muse: The Inner Lives of Women: A World Poetry Anthology*, edited by Kate Rogers and Viki Holmes, Haven Books, Hong Kong, 2009. (28)

Barreno, Maria Isabel; Horta, Maria Teresa; da Costa, Maria Velho, in *A Book of Women Poets from Antiquity to Now*, edited by Aliki Barnstone and Willis Barnstone, Shocken Books, New York, 1992. (39)

Barskova, Polina, *The Zoo in Winter: Selected Poems*, selected and translated by Boris Dralyuk and David Stromberg, Melville House, Brooklyn, New York, 2010. (60)

Bishop, Elizabeth, *The Complete Poems 1927–1979*, Farrar, Straus and Giroux, New York, 1983. (19, 32)

Boland, Eavan, *New Collected Poems*, W.W. Norton & Company, New York & London, 2009. (10, 13, 14, 16, 31, 36, 38)

Briggs, Rachael, 'Steep Tea', a renga. (55)

Bridge, Diana, *Aloe and Other Poems*, Auckland University Press, Auckland, 2009. (50)

Cai, Yan, in *A Book of Women Poets from Antiquity to Now*, edited by Aliki Barnstone and Willis Barnstone, Schocken Books, New York, 1992. (41)

di Michele, Mary, *The Flower of Youth: Pier Paolo Pasolini Poems*, ECW Press, Toronto, 2011. (59)

Graham, Jorie, *The Dream of the Unified Field: Selected Poems 1974–1994*, Harper Collins, New York, 2002. (26)

Hale, Sarah Josepha, *Poems for Our Children*, Marsh, Capen & Lyon, Boston, 1830. (29)

Hameed, Yasmeen, in *Modern Poetry of Pakistan*, edited by Iftikhar Arif, translations edited by Waqas Khwaja, Dalkey Archive Press, Champaign and London, 2010. (65)

Khalvati, Mimi, in *Villanelles*, edited by Annie Finch and Marie-Elizabeth Mali, Everyman's Library Pocket Poets, Alfred A. Knopf, New York, London, and Toronto, 2012. (37)

Kimura, Nobuko, in *Japanese Women Poets: An Anthology*, edited by Hiroaki Sato, M.E. Sharpe, Inc., New York, 2008. (25)

Lanyer, Aemilia, in *Isabella Whitney, Mary Sidney and Aemilia Lanyer: Renaissance Women Poets*, edited by Danielle Clarke, Penguin Books, London, 2000. (9)

Lee, Tzu Pheng, *Prospect of a Drowning*, Heinemann Educational Books (Asia) Ltd, 1980; *Against the Next Wave*, Times Books International, 1988; *The Brink of an Amen*, Times Books International, 1991; *Lambada by Galilee and Other Surprises*, Times Editions Pte Ltd, 1997; and in *Over*

There: Poems from Singapore and Australia, edited by John Kinsella and Alvin Pang, Ethos Books, Singapore, 2008. (17, 34, 44, 46, 51)

Leong, Liew Geok, in *Over There: Poems from Singapore and Australia*, edited by John Kinsella and Alvin Pang, Ethos Books, Singapore, 2008. (62)

Li, Qingzhao, *Complete Poems*, translated by Kenneth Rexroth and Ling Chung, New Directions, New York, 1980. (52)

Ní Chuilleanáin, Eiléan, *Selected Poems*, Gallery Books (Oldcastle, Ireland) and Faber and Faber (London), 2008. (12, 40, 47)

Ni', Xunka' Utz'utz', in *Incantations: Songs, Spells and Images by Mayan Women*, edited by Ámbar Past, with Xalik Guzmán Bakbolom and Xpetra Ernandes, Cinco Puntos Press, El Paso, 2005. (20)

okpik, dg nanouk, in *Effigies: An Anthology of New Indigenous Writing, Pacific Rim, 2009*, edited by Allison Adelle Hedge Coke, Salt Publishing, Cambridge, UK, 2009. (49)

Oliver, Mary, *House of Light*, Beacon Press, Boston, 1990. (45)

Pitter, Ruth, *Collected Poems*, Enitharmon Press, London, 1996. (23)

Ryan, Kay, *The Niagara River*, Grove Press, New York, 2005. (15)

Sachs, Nelly, *Collected Poems 1944–1949*, translated by Michael Hamburger, Ruth and Matthew Mead, and Michael Roloff, Green Integer, Copenhagen and Los Angeles, 2011. (30)

Smith, Charlotte, in *Eighteenth-Century Women Poets*, edited by Roger Lonsdale, Oxford University Press, USA, 1990. (63)

Teasdale, Sara, *The Collected Poems of Sara Teasdale*, Collier Books, New York, 1966. (27)

Tostó, Munda, in *Incantations: Songs, Spells and Images by Mayan Women*, edited by Ámbar Past, with Xalik Guzmán Bakbolom and Xpetra Ernandes, Cinco Puntos Press, El Paso, 2005. (18)

Traditional, in *A Book of Women Poets from Antiquity to Now*, edited by Aliki Barnstone and Willis Barnstone, Shocken Books, New York, 1992. (48)

Wickham, Anna, *The Writings of Anna Wickham: Free Woman and Poet*, edited and introduced by R.D. Smith, Virago Press, London, 1984; and *Anna Wickham: A Poet's Daring Life*, by Jennifer Vaughan Jones, Madison Books, London, New York, and Oxford, 2003. (11)

Wroth, Lady Mary, *The Poems of Lady Mary Wroth*, edited with an introduction and notes by Josephine A. Roberts, Louisiana State University Press, Baton Rouge and London, 1983. (24)

Yamada, Mizue, in *Japanese Women Poets: An Anthology*, edited by Hiroaki Sato, M.E. Sharpe, Inc., New York, 2008. (54)

Zhang, Er, *So Translating Rivers and Cities*, translated with the author by Bob Holman, Arpine Konyalian Grenier, Timothy Liu, Bill Ransom, Susan M. Schultz and Leonard Schwartz, Zephyr Press, Brookline MA, 2007. (22)